811.6 Fra
Francis, TaKasha L.
The diva's diary : original poetic
thought : notes and commentary
on l

34028073707508
CC ocn499058418
01/15/10

WITHDRAWN

Barbara Bush Library Friends
Building a better library — *one book at a time.*

Donated By

E.B.O.N.Y.

THE DIVA'S DIARY:

Original poetic thought-notes and commentary on love and life-

Volume I

TaKasha L. Francis

Copyright © 2008 by TaKasha L. Francis, Esq.

Printed in the United States of America

ISBN 1-978-1-60458-308-3

All rights reserved solely by the author. The author guarantees all contents are original and do not infringe upon the legal rights of any other person or work. No part of this book may be used or reproduced by any means, graphic, electronic, or mechanical, including photocopying, recording, taping, or by any information storage retrieval system without written permission of the publisher except in the case of brief quotations embodied in critical articles and reviews.

Scripture quotations marked KJV have been taken from the King James Bible.

The quoted ideas expressed in this book (but not scripture verses) are not, in all cases, exact quotations, as some have been edited for clarity and brevity. In all cases, the author has attempted to maintain the speaker's original intent. In some cases, quoted material for this book was obtained from secondary sources. While every effort was made to ensure the accuracy of these sources, the accuracy cannot be guaranteed.

∞ The Dedication ∞

To HIM,

who blessed me with such beautiful gifts to be used to His glory,

and whose gifts have, and will continue to make room for me,

who told me that through HIM, ALL things are possible

and this step of faith is just the beginning………

I love you Father.

A man's gift maketh room for him, and bringeth him before great men.

Proverbs 18:16 (KJV)

∞ A note from the author ∞

"The pen is the tongue of the mind."

-Horace

What you're about to read is a very personal work and a serious step of faith for me. I decided to publish my poetry last spring after a divine encounter with a sister named Veronica Reaux. After performing my signature piece "DIVA" at the 2007 Mmasacheba Women's Retreat, Veronica and many of the sisters were blessed and empowered by the piece. They approached me to purchase copies of the poem and their requests planted a seed in my mind to create a poster print of my work. However, Veronica's desire to hang a copy of DIVA in her hair salon moved this idea from "thought" to "action". She went on to tell me she'd be proud to post a copy of "DIVA" in her hair salon. Her request humbled me. Since writing is cathartic for me, I saw my writing as just a therapeutic past time. Veronica and the sisters on that retreat helped me realize that my poetry inspired and encouraged people the same way it encouraged and inspired me. It was time to share some of my private thoughts publicly and allow my gift to be a blessing to others.

I began compiling pieces I'd written from old journals that I'd kept. As I re-read my journals I re-lived some exciting and painful memories. God told me to include some of my personal entries to free myself and bless others by sharing some of my experiences. I reluctantly began this work. The more I worked on it, the more I started to back up from this assignment because it was becoming too personal and in some instances, too painful. But the Father also reminded me that this is a great opportunity to bless others. Somebody, somewhere, is going through or has been through what I've been through. They need to know they're not alone and that they can overcome. Someone needs to be inspired to do more, be more and go where they never thought possible. While others need to just maintain their sanity. Someone needs to know its okay not to be perfect and that we all mess up and sometimes fail. Someone needs to laugh to keep from crying, and someone simply needs to let go and cry. Don't be alarmed when you encounter "less than Godly" language. Christians cuss too☺ This is <u>REAL TALK</u>!

I am reminded of my friend Linda Reece's words to me years ago, "Whatever you go through in life is never for you; it's always for someone else." With that being said, what you're about to read are bits and pieces of some situations in my life and what I've observed in the lives of others. These are snippets of what I've been through for you....my best days and my worst, my highs and my lows, my triumphs, and my failures. You'll laugh, cry, reminisce, say "Amen!" and "That's right!" But most importantly, you'll be blessed! The secrets are finally out!

THE DIVA'S DIARY
Poetic thought-notes on love and life-Volume I

The Diva on Love and Relationships

Mood: Cool
The Diary Intro……………………………………….3

Mood: Amorous
In my eyes……………………………………….11
What I Like……………………………….....………15
I think I love you……………………………………. .17
Just caught myself ……………………………….. 20
How Far ……………………………………........ 21

Mood: Enraged
You Didn't Have to Lie……………....……………… 27
Too much, too soon ……………......………………… 29

Mood: Blah
Dear breeze……………………………………………… 37
Lonely…………………………………………….......… 38

Mood: Vexed
Mad as HELL!!!! ………………………………….……….43

Mood: Hopeful
The ONE ………………......……………………….....51
A few words from the heart ………………………53

Mood: Disgusted
You don't know me……………………………………60

The Diva on Life
Mood: Contemplative
Different..69
Searchin'...70
A New Day..72
Thoughts that run amuck 73

Mood: Sassy
DIVA 81

Mood: Angry
God Ain't Sleep 87
The Knockout 89

Mood: Crunk!
Go Get It!...97
I see it! 98
And So We Commence 100

Mood: Depressed
Accept..107

Mood: Reflective
(In loving memory of Grandmama)
Legacy 112
Enjoying the Journey............................113
I Watched You Sleep 118

Mood: Introspective
A Battered Woman's Plight..................125

A Tribute to the Sorors
So You Want to be a Delta?..................131

Mood: Cool

"One thing only I know, and that is that I know nothing."
Socrates

I'm sitting in Starbucks looking cosmopolitan, sipping my latte, about to record my thoughts in my newest little friend. It's been a while since I've kept a journal. I really don't like journaling as much as I used to but I can't afford therapy at the moment. (smile) I know this is supposed to be therapeutic, but I don't know if I want my innermost thoughts available in print. Heaven forbid if anyone gets their hands on it ☺ I'm not even sure what I'm supposed to be writing about. My feelings? The day's events? God's purpose for me in life? It's hard to tell. Anyhoo, this may help me become a better person, so here goes...

♥ *LOVE* ♥

Mood: Amorous

"Sometimes you have not even begun to speak - and I am at the end of what you are saying."
(Kahlil Gibran from Mary Haskell's Journal. July 28, 1917.)

I still haven't quite figured him out. He stares at me a lot. I wonder what he's thinking about. I want to ask him but I'm not sure if he'll tell me. He's definitely the strong, silent type. Like so many men, he's so closed with his feelings. I'll probably never know. Maybe he doesn't know how to tell me what he's feeling. I sense he cares about me a lot… it's as if his eyes say what his lips cannot. We feel so good together. The chemistry is overwhelming at times. He's my peace, and I am his. He looks like burdens literally lift off his shoulders when he walks through my door. I could be like this with him forever. We're connected on a level that's indescribable. There really are no words. I love the fact that we look into each other's eyes a lot. It's so intimate…more so than some of the best physical experiences I've had. It's deeper. I like it because that's not something you can do with everyone. It's at those times I feel so close to him. But I still want to know what he's thinking…

IN MY EYES

What do you see when you look into my eyes?

Do you see how much you mean to me?

How much I care

Or do you see nothing while you stare?

Do you see how I miss you desperately when you're away?

Do you see how I think of you everyday?

Do you see my heart leaping or my reaction to your touch?

Do you see how strong my feelings are because I care for you so much?

A mixture of awe and contemplation it seems

Is this how I look inside your dreams?

You don't talk much about your feelings for me,

But your actions say they may be deep

I don't know if even you can articulate what you feel when we meet

When you look into my eyes and stare,

do you see me fighting between "like" and "love" feelings?

Wanting to say "I love you"

but scared because your heart may not also be there

Do you see my soul cry when you're hurt?

Do you truly see my beauty and inner worth?

I know you think I'm pretty

But still you can't disguise

The feelings we both feel

When we look into each others eyes…

Tonight he asked me what I like. The way I'm feeling right now, that's the wrong question to ask me (lol). All that did was put sex on the brain. I mean, he is so sexy. And it's getting harder and harder to resist him. Sometimes I feel like goin' for it and just asking for forgiveness later! Being celibate ain't <u>no joke</u>. I wanna live right, but Lord it gets hard on a sista. I know I need to pray or read some scripture or something, but honestly, I don't want to stop thinking about it. Mama says to pray and ask God to take these desires away until I get married. I ain't tryin' to hear none of that either right now. I want to imagine... re-live...create and re-create some great moments. Besides God has a funny way of giving us what we ask for and may turn me into a prude. Humph, the devil is a lie! (lol) But seriously, why would God give us these feelings and then require us not to act on them? Hell, if I can't get it, I ought to be able to think about it... right?

WHAT I LIKE

You asked me last night
What I like
I told you we'd talk later
But these things came to my mind
I like romance
Flowers, cards, and little gifts just because
Long passionate kisses and strong lingering hugs
Fingers touching, exploring my body gently
Cuddling against your chest
listening to your heartbeat
the sound of your voice before I lay down at night
telling me you miss me, or just
checkin' with me to see if my day is going right.
Staring deep into my eyes,
telling me what's on your mind
Sharing your innermost thoughts, dreams, and feelings
Someone who shares my sorrows and pain
and there's nothing like the sound of your voice calling my name
I like being pampered and spoiled
A massage or foot rub will do
I like doors held open, my hand being held,
And a compliment or two
I like the smell of a man
Wearing his favorite cologne
I like fresh breath that lingers
Long after the kiss is gone
I like someone touching my face
The way you did last night
Face serene, mind at peace
I wonder if I'm in your dreams,
Behind your lids, a beautiful scene,
I like watching your chest go up and down
As you slightly snore, stretch, and turn around,
Uhmm, you look so cute when you sleep,

I like
how throughout the night,
you reach for me,
To embrace me tenderly,
I like how good you feel…
So right…
Your innocence overwhelms me in your slumber
Just being near you, intoxicates me and takes me under,
I like the sound of thunder
And rain tapping on my windowpane,
Creating love scenes with you
that would make Zane shame,
Until the rising of the next morning's sun
To the groove of Mechelle Ndegeocello's "Love Song #1"…
I like that you want to know what I like
Making me a priority
Showing sensitivity……..
Hmmm… I'm excited at the possibilities…..

I THINK I LOVE YOU

I think I love you
I think about you all the time,
Replaying our last meeting over and over in my mind
Looking forward to the next,
Anxious to embrace you
and find sweet rest upon your chest
I –think- I…… .
love you
Just the thought of you makes me smile
a child,
is what I turn into
when I'm with you
You become "Daddy"
instead of my "boo"
I adore the "Father" in you
Willing to let you protect me, lead me, guide me, provide for me,
And do all the things a man should do,
Damn I-
think I-
love you,
You excite me beyond words,
I want to sit at your feet,
I don't even care what you're saying baby,
I just love to hear you **talk** to me,
Magic happens when you speak,
Your wisdom astounds me,
Your knowledge confounds me,
Your mind knows no boundaries,
My heart can't stop pounding
Because I-
think I-
love you.

There's something about the way you look at me,
That makes me feel like the most beautiful girl you've ever seen,
As if you can't wait to go to sleep
to see me in your dreams,
Boosting my self esteem,
you treat me like a queen,
because in your eyes,
nothing in this world is too good for me.
And while other women walk by
they don't even catch your eye
because a vision of me
is all you see,
driving me crazy
when you say my body is "amazing"----
and why others try
doesn't even phase me
because I
think I
love you baby.
I've gone back to seventh grade
pickin' out his and hers baby names
for the children I want to have for you,
Swollen feet, morning sickness and all
no order is too great or too tall,
to bring forth the result of the ultimate collab with you,
And I thought I knew
what love was before you,
But I don't just think I love you boo,
I simply adore you!
I want to make you happy at any cost
I want to be the reason you smile and the glide in your stride,
I'm willing to let you be the boss,
Play my part, and humbly step aside.
I don't know what has come over me
But deep within my heart rings true,
A feeling beyond desirable

And downright undeniable
I think I love you...

JUST CAUGHT MYSELF

Just caught myself thinking about you

Your smile

Your touch

Your scent

Your kiss

The bliss I feel

when you

Hold me

Caress me

Lie next to me

The sound of your voice

The way that you care

Running my fingers through your hair

Listening to your heartbeat as I lay on your chest

Just caught myself thinking about you

Hopefully thinking of me too

HOW FAR?

How far would you go for love?
Would you climb the highest mountain?
Swim the deepest sea?
Live a thousand centuries?
Or give your life for me?

If love slapped you in the face, would you recognize it?
Would you embrace it?
Or run in the other direction?
Would you accept my love,
or toy with my intense affections?

If love stopped you on the street and said hello
Would you carry on a conversation and act interested?
Or would you leave love standing there, desolate and alone,
feeling dissed again?
If love told you to jump,
Would you sit there like a lump,
or stand there and wonder "Why?"
Or would you simply ask "How high?"
Before jumping towards the sky?

How far would you go for love?
Do you think it's worth it?
Or is it something you choose to forget?
Is death the only thing that could keep you from it?

When you see love, fervently pursue it
Don't shun it, and act as if you never knew it
Embrace it and make it your own at any cost
Or
Throw it away, and later on mourn the loss.

Mood: Enraged!!!

"Betrayal teaches that you can survive anything. All the things you thought you couldn't handle, you can."
Oprah Winfrey

Rage!!!!!

That's all I feel when I think of how he lied to me. He looked me in my face and lied to me like it was easy....without flinching, fidgeting, or a modicum of conscious. I gave him a chance to tell me the truth, but instead he lied and took my choice away! Because of his selfish, triflin' ass, I'm the other woman! I've never been on this side of the fence and I am so not feelin' the disrespect! I know part of the reason he lied is because I told him from the beginning I don't deal with men in relationships. He assured me he wasn't in one. Knowing that, why didn't he just go on to someone else? There are plenty of women who don't mind being the side piece. If he liked me that much, he could have broken off the relationship he was in and come correct. Hell, I've never played second to anyone. I'm good enough to be the ONLY one. All this time, I'm thinking what we had was special and he was lying to me. What's worse...I believed him.

The messed up part is that as mad as I am right now, I know what we had was special. It makes me madder that I wasn't imagining what we felt for each other. I wasn't just a chick on the side to him. Those feelings were deep and real. So now I've invested time and energy into something that can't go anywhere. I'm so depressed right now thinking about him and how he's going on with his life. Like I don't even freakin' exist. I bet he doesn't even think of the pain he's caused me. All I kept seeing today were images of him with her...touching her...being with her.... That was us together! That should be us together!!! That's what he said he wanted!!!! So why am I miserable, trying to hold on to my mind, and choking back tears while he's happy as hell doing what he wants to do with her and clearly everyone else? Dammit I hate him! He didn't have to lie.

YOU DIDN'T HAVE TO LIE

What started as hello
Now ends in good bye,
because
You didn't have to lie
Wasn't even interested at first
But now I like you
and it hurts
 because
You didn't have to lie
I don't know why you even took that route
Because it was nothing to lie about
We were just hanging out as friends,
Nothing exclusive
Just doin'
Me and you
on an occasional weekend,
But then those weekends turned into daily texts
calls from work and midnight chats
Holding hands, hugs, and first kiss,
Asking me if it was you that I miss,
Catching feelings I changed my mind
Deciding it was with you I wanted to spend my time,
but
You didn't have to lie
As we got closer, you came over to my place,
Sucked up my air conditioning
and took up my space,
Parked your feet under a table already made
with your favorite meal
and a glass of lemonade
Dang boy, I like you!
I'm cooking your meals
packing leftovers for your lunch
and massagin' your heels,

Thinking of us together, no longer just friends
Ready to tell other brothas
 "Whatever! "
 To the left boo-boo!
This is where it ends,
So when I ask you if you are committed, back and forth, married or otherwise,
You looked me in my face

And told me
 a lie
A lie you could have kept and saved me all this mess
Lying like a pro,
Makin' me your sideline ho?
But I'm like Bee
If I can't be everything, then I'll be nothing at all,
You got back with her
and had the nerve to call
and tell me
"I like you ", "I miss you", "I've been thinking about you" and "I care"
After all the wonderful moments
and quality time we've shared?
You ask, "Can we be friends?"
Yeah brotha,
We can be friends,
just not with each other,
It's been real,
but now its goodbye,
because
you simply didn't have to lie.

TOO MUCH, TOO SOON

Looking for love

Latching on to whatever I find

Endlessly searching for a love that's mine

Why don't these relationships work?

Why don't they last?

Why am I constantly haunted by the ghosts of my past?

So what?

I let him know I like him

Started answering his calls

Wanting to spend time with him

And give him my all

Inviting him to my house

Cooking him a few meals

Allowing him to stay over

My soul I started to reveal

So what?

I started communicating

How much I missed him

And wanted to be near him

How I longed for his touch

How he was growing on me, making me want him so much

Writing poetry for this man

Making him my muse

On my mind

All the time

More than those other dudes

Too much too soon

The script got flipped

Now I'm the one pursuing him

Waiting on his call

Catering to his every whim

Recalling past moments and fantasizing of moments to come

Went from not feeling you to thinking

"He may be the one"

My mindset changed

A girlfriend I became

Without out discussion or remark

Little did I know, he was seeping out from my head

Into my heart,

The start

Of something new, forever and true

But no…

It was simply, too much, too soon

So now what do I do?

Caught up, entangled in his spell,

One minute floatin' in heaven

The next dying in hell

Emotions –confusing

Feelings all over the place

A downward spiral we are because now there's no chase…..

You got me where you want me and that's

In love with you…

All because I gave up

too much

too soon

Mood:

Blah

"Relax, relate, release..."

Whitley Gilbert (A Different World-1987)

Feels nice out here tonight. Nice and breezy. Hmmm... I miss him. Does he miss me? This is the kind of night we should be spending together. I mean the sky is perfect.....dark and littered with itty bitty stars twinkling in the night. The kind of sky lovers should stand under staring into each other's eyes. The kind of sky that witnessed him telling me he loves me, and only wants to be with me and no one else. Instead it is witnessing a woman alone and broken hearted. There goes that breeze again. I wonder where else it's blowing tonight. Ewww...mosquitoes are out...guess they want to spend the night out here too (lol) But it really is a beautiful night.

DEAR BREEZE

Dear breeze
Where are you going?
Teasing me, caressing my skin
As you blow by
Dear breeze
where are you coming from?
The balcony of two lovers holding each other in love's embrace?
The side of a road where a hitchhiker waves down a ride into the unknown?
Through the window of a broken family as an exhausted wife and mother waits for her husband to come home?
Dear breeze,
Won't you stay awhile?
Let me bask in you
Encircle me like the arms that no longer hold me
Kiss me like the lips I miss immensely
Whisper a song of enchantment and love that seems so long ago
This beautiful summer night
Romance me like the days of old.
You've always been there during my most beautiful moments
Dear breeze,
Whipping, whisking, and whooshing, through my hair and clothes as I contemplate life and what it all means
My quiet times, you were there
Whispering,
 whispering,
Dear breeze
Where are you going?
 Where will I meet you next?

LONELY

Whatever happens to the love that exists between two people that finally find each other?
Does it go away to hide?
Can time truly take away the pain that you feel inside?
Why does everything always have to change?
Why do I find myself lonely again?

Time only manifests itself in those who choose to live…
Live every single day to the fullest
What have I done so wrong?
Why must I suffer all alone?
Is there really someone out there for me to love and to love me too?
Or will there be more changes for me to go through?

Lonely
That's how it seems it's gonna be
That's how I feel
As the days go by
The reality of it becomes more and more real

Will this feeling ever go away, or just keep repeating itself

Listen to me, and let me tell you what I know
Listen to the words of my heart, and watch my emotions flow
Listen to my heart break, every time they go away
Listen to the tears roll, as in rolls another day…

Mood:

Vexed

"Your playing small does not serve the world. There is nothing enlightened about shrinking so that other people won't feel insecure around you."

Marianne Williamson

Today a friend emailed me this article by a sista that feels like black women are scaring off their men and that's why most of us are still single. We're too independent and headstrong for our own good, and while that may work in the board room, it does not work in the home.

My initial thought after reading this is how tired I am of "black women" being blamed for their single state. Truth is, most independent and accomplished women want to take care of their men and do so, more often than we think. But when you've done that for men who have proven they aren't worthy, a sista decides to do what she knows works in other areas of her life. Furthermore, where are the Cliff Huxtables and Barack Obamas that glory and bask in their wives' intelligence and strength? Adhering to today's standards, my only hope for the man I deserve is to "dumb-down" and cater to his ego. No thank you! The blatant hypocrisy in the notion that black women like us are scaring off our men because of traits that make us attractive to them and successful in other areas is incongruous. This is an example of the misogyny that perpetuates the idea that women are subservient and quite frankly, I'm tired of it.

Furthermore, in 1 Corinthians, God defines love in pertinent part as follows, "Love always protects, always trusts, always hopes, always perseveres." In my opinion, more women have mastered this concept than men because we tolerate more than a little bit to keep our families and relationships together. We accept them at their worst and endure trials that would make ordinary women lose their minds. We love them and accept them "flaws and all." However, it seems that rather than persevere and love us "flaws and all", most men opt to move around much earlier in the game. So, a large part of the problem is that the men we are "scaring" choose not to persevere.

Why? Because they don't have to. They have more than enough suitable options within and across races to choose from, while black women are stuck with trying to make it work with the remnant of our limited selection which includes felons, miscreants, homosexuals, bi-sexuals, whoremongers and womanizers, infidels, lazy and trifling men who won't support their families, successful brothas with attitudes, "interracial" tendencies, or "Oedipus complexes", and the list goes on and on. It takes two to make a relationship work and while black women could make some adjustments, I honestly think we compromise enough. So tag brothas, you're it!!!

MAD AS HELL

I'm not bitter,
I'm mad as hell,
Giving my all and the relationship fails
I know I'm the common denominator and played my part,
But all this bull ain't on me,
I'm the one with the broken heart,
Seems like when you treat em' nice and treat em' right,
They take you for granted like they're God's gift,
Dishin' out more and more of their respective bull*ish
To test you to see how much you can take,
To see if you'll stick around yet another day,
So many tests,
So many hoops,
Why you're testing me brotha,
 I should be testing you.
You wanna make sure I'm no golddigga,
So you do the bare minimum, if anything at all,
You wanna make sure I'm down for you, so you sleep with me, and then barely call,
You wanna make sure I got your back, so you act a fool and talk smack when the reality is, you ain't all that,
And why I choose to spend time with you has nothing to do with desperation boo,
I'm tryin' to give a brotha a chance with yo' no money-havin', think he's a playa, mama's boy, insecure, confused selfish, undeserving ass,
In reality you're trash,
but I wanted to find your treasure,
I've always known that I deserve, can have, and have had better,
But I didn't want to be accused of passing up a good man not packaged the way I'd expected,
Now fooling with you, I'm the one that's rejected,
It makes me cry and I ask myself why the relationships don't work,
In some cases, I've given too much, too soon,

in others, I haven't given enough,
It seems I haven't found a middle ground
that makes me soft, yet tough
I may not look or act like it
but I want and need love too,
I want to feel it all through me
and be the best woman to you,
But you want to use me for my money, my sex, or whatever other benefit you can get,
Ready to tell me "to the left" when I regain my self-respect and put you in check,
Moving on or continuing, shall I say,
with some other stupid female who lets you have your way,
Had "filet mignon",
but a "tuna-fish" sandwich is where you'd rather be,
Not with someone who clearly makes you better,
But with someone who hangs on your every word
and spells them out letter by letter,
You're not worried about someone who is strong and true,
You simply want someone who is impressed with you,
Well impressed I am not,
Now that the truth is out,
I'm mad as hell because I wasted my time,
Became vulnerable and you played with my mind
I know I'll get over this,
And as days go by,
You'll think about me and miss
My beautiful face, my gorgeous smile,
My intelligent, substantive conversation,
My classy style,
My cozy place,
My "slap yo mama'" food,
The sound of my voice loving and encouraging you,
My kindness and my thoughtfulness
My drive and ambition prompting you to love and want life's best,
My sense of humor, and my touch,

See what happens when you mess up? You miss out on so much.
You may not see it now, or you could be full of regret,
But I am one special lady you won't ever forget.
Before me there were none and after me there will be no more,
And for the record, all I've got over here for you is a closed door-
Slammed shut to your lies, your games, your disrespect,
There will be no more chances to get me caught up in that,
I've got an icebox where my heart used to be,
Thrown away the lock and the key so no one else can hurt me,
Maybe some day, the ice will melt and my heart will be free,
Free to be with someone truly deserving of me,
We'll see…

Mood:

Hopeful

"Let him kiss me with the kisses of his mouth: for thy love is better than wine."
Song of Solomon 1:2 (KJV)

Everyone says love will come when you least expect it. Now I'm a believer! From the moment we met, I knew he was special. There was something different about him. Ironically, he said the same thing about me! How freaky is that??? Since then, I marvel at what a "God send" this man is! He is everything I've prayed for and from what he tells me the feeling is mutual. We have so much in common. It's almost like he's a male version of me. Whenever we talk, we end up talking for hours. But it's not mindless chit-chat. The conversation is so good, we don't even notice how late the hour is, or the fact that we've been talking so long. It's like we never run out of things to talk about and we have talked nearly everyday since our fist date. It's like we've known each other for years.

And he is such an incredible person! He's saved...for real (lol) HALLELUJAH!!!! He values his relationship with God and makes it a priority, and I love it! He's so kind, honorable, and sweet. He is goofy and he makes me laugh. His laugh alone cracks me up because he's so silly. Seeing him laugh is even funnier. His eyes totally disappear (lol) But its so cute though ☺ He's handsome, considerate, intelligent, cultured and more than I could have known to ask for. A true gentleman. Every day since we met I've been checking off things on my four page list for my mate. Ahhhh......I haven't been this happy in a while because I think I've finally encountered an equal yoke. I feel like God has finally honored my faith and sent me the mate I deserve. I believe He sent me the counterpart He promised me if I would obey and trust Him. It's about time! I think I've finally met someone that gets me. Someone who appreciates me and isn't intimidated. Someone who digs my intelligence and will be encouraging and supportive. The time we've spent together has been extraordinary and I simply <u>ADORE</u> him. I just ADORE him! Although it's early, I think he may finally be the one.....

THE ONE

Could you be the one?
The one I've prayed for and never thought would come
Everyone told me you'd show up when I least expected it
And while I know I deserve this blessing
I thought I'd never get it
Wow! You really amaze me!
Are you even real?
Better yet, are you for real?
I can't believe you are so thoughtful, considerate, and kind,
You touched me in a place more intimate than others have experienced
Brotha, you've already made love to my mind,
With your intellect, your care, your sincerity,
And the thought of you loving me fills me with glee
Because I feel you'd never want to hurt me,
Not just because of me,
But because it would hurt you too much,
I see you placing my needs before yours,
Showering me with tokens of love and opening doors
 A total gentleman, you're shaping up to be,
A blessing from God
 tailor made for me
If you're what I think,
You've made up for all the drama, tears, bitterness, and my broken heart
I'm scared because I don't want to bring this baggage into a new situation
Being with you is a new start
This is different
I can feel it
I don't feel like I need to play the games I used to play
Like not calling, not being available or acting disinterested,
I want to give you my time
and reap the reward of it being well invested

I feel like,
 should I love you down the line,
I'll be able to do so freely
Without fear of getting hurt,
or of wasting my time
I feel like my season of loneliness is coming to an end
God has sent me a wonderful-
very special-
 beautiful-
 friend.

A FEW WORDS FROM THE HEART

How I feel about you,
is more than mere words can explain
It is a beautiful feeling that envelopes me
whenever I hear you call my name
You call to me
 like a smooth, tranquil voice floating softly in the wind
Beckoning me to come to you
Close to you
Beside you
To become one with you
To become joined with you... one spirit to another

I love you...
words spoken by a true King
to the Queen who adores you
supports you
 needs you
loves you...
The true Queen who stands tall right beside you
in your heart
in your mind
and in your soul.

Hold me
Close to your heart
Keep me
Deep in your thoughts
Respect me
As I will always respect you
Cherish me
And to you, I will always be true
Honor me
To keep our relationship strong
Trust me
Be assured that I would not do you wrong

Comfort me
Whenever I need a friend
Love me
And adore me forever,
until the end

Mood:

Disgusted

"Never make someone a priority that makes you an option."

Unknown

"Don't make someone a priority that makes you an option". I don't know who coined this phrase, but it's powerful. Whew! That says it all. There's nothing worse than being in a relationship by yourself just to say you have a "man"-even if it's in name only. We have men in our beds and on our arms that are only there physically. Their minds are clearly somewhere else-whether it's another chick or the game on T.V. They aren't giving 100% and everybody, including you, knows it. It's sad. We're in it to win it, but the brotha could take or leave the situation. You're taken for granted in the worst way and all you can do is feel your heart hurt because you're living a lie. You see your self esteem crumble right before your eyes because you really do know who you are and what you have to offer; yet you wonder why <u>this</u> man doesn't see it. Bit by bit, it eats away at you until you start to believe you can't do any better. You prefer to deal with the "devil" you know, rather than the one you don't. That's a hurtful place, but today's dating game leaves many of us in that situation. Having been there, I have no desire to experience that again. If this is the only option, I'll continue diggin' my own space.

Even when they say they want to be friends, we think we can handle it because deep down we think we can change them. That's the biggest lie ever told. Only God can change people-if there's a willing heart. We figure a piece of him is better than none of him if we cut him off. Friends before lovers, right? Instead we allow them to emotionally use us, because while they are not ready to fully commit, they want to keep us around. I ended up getting more hurt by sticking around and wasting valuable time waiting on someone that didn't want me, instead of investing it in someone who did. Someone once said, "When you waste my time, you waste my life." Nuff said.

Men know what they want and how to express themselves if they feel strongly enough about you. I learned the hard way that if he's not making you a priority, he really doesn't see you as one. No matter how busy we are, we make time for what is important to us. If you're really what he wants, you'll know it because of how well he treats you. That's why I told him we can't be friends. A piece of me died inside when he said that's all he wanted. I felt like I'd been hit by a car...over and over again...because I thought he was different...I thought this was different. I mean, if friendship is all you wanted, what have we been doing all this time? So I had a hard decision to make...I let him go. If it's God's will, we'll have another shot at it. But it's certainly not God's will for me to convince him I'm the one for him. The one God has for me will know it and act like he knows it. This conversation won't even be necessary.

People say whenever you see a sista that's got it goin' on and single, she's single because she's crazy. While that's true in some cases, it's not the reason most of us are single. One of the main reasons I think is because so often people treat the uncommon like its common. What I'm realizing is that some men don't realize what a wonderful blessing we are. Or they do realize it and don't know what to do with us. They're scared or intimidated. Some men say they're scared because there were so many areas they feel they can't lead us in. They need to feel "needed". Others say women like me require much more work and they're not ready to put in the time. It's easier dating women who didn't require as much. What's funny is most of us don't even think about these things. One of the most important things I need from my man is to be my rock. Sometimes I want to be able to lean on someone else since everyone leans on me. Someone to wipe my tears and tell me everything's gonna be okay. That doesn't cost a thing and they can't do that either. They don't know us. They don't recognize us as the Queens that we are. I talked to Minister Jackie and she broke it down to me. She says only a King can recognize a Queen, and a Queen can't mate with a jack. (Hah!) She told me I was looking for a "Boaz", and hung up on a "jack-ass". (lol) Dang! Is that "what had happened????' (lol) Hmmmmm...freeing thought...

YOU DON'T KNOW ME

You don't know me,
You see my exterior,
The trappings, the finery,
You know I'm someone special
Because the strength of my presence dictates such
You're drawn to me because of curiosity,
What makes me tick,
And why I'm so fabulous
But what you can see
 isn't what makes me the tea,
It's God's hand on me
that makes me a queen,
I am chosen
set apart
unusual
and distinct
And when I say you don't know me
It's not a cliché,
Or some over the top "diva-tude" on display
It's knowing the goodness of my heart
and the gentleness of my soul,
My fiery opinionated moments
and my quiet control
The love that I possess and want to share
With open arms of someone who really wants to be there
But you turn away, out of intimidation and fear,
Knowing where you are, but my expectations are up here,
Taking the easy route, cause it's an easy out-
Not willing to put in work with the ultimate
But willing to settle with what's easy
and not hard to get
You regret
It every time you think about what you've lost,
You should've thought harder about it

You should have counted the cost
And even though it's your loss
I can't help but toss
around the idea of what could've been,
had I lowered my standards
and accepted what little you were offerin'
It's discouragin'
On this throne
Because I'm often here alone
holding out for quality
While I'm seeking Boaz,
I'm caught up on a jack ass,
And a jack can never mate with a Queen
Only a King is a suitable fit
And while they all may not have been it
I implore God, why me??????
I'm glad to be set apart
Because I have a place in His heart
But the isolation is killing me!
I stew in misery
Wondering if there's anyone out there for me...
To love me, not hurt me,
Someone truly worthy of creating a dynasty of our kingdom breed....
What is it about them that make them go another way?
Or pursue me at first and decide not to stay?

♦ LIFE ♦

Mood:

Contemplative

"The heaviest burden to bear is that of great potential."

Unknown

Sometimes I wish I could be like everyone else. I envy people who just do and say whatever they want. It's like they live without a conscious and they seem to have more fun. I'm not perfect, but I always feel like I'm living under a heavenly recorder. I'm always thinking about doing the right thing and try to do that most of the time. When I don't do what's right, I feel super-duper guilty. I hate having a conscious sometimes. Sometimes I just want to let go!!!!! Hang loose!!!!! It seems like there's a freedom in not having one. Yeah there are consequences, but it still seems like more fun.

I've always known I was different. As a child I didn't think, act, or speak like most kids. I didn't like being different because people made fun of me then, and still do. But now I understand that being "different" is a mark of distinction from God. What I thought was "different" was simply God showing me I was "Chosen". I'm special, not strange. I'm set apart, not second rate. I'm not like everyone else and neither was Jesus. He saved all humanity. I can only imagine what God has planned for me to do.

DIFFERENT

As God looked over all He made,
An entire flock of sheep,
He said, "I want that one."
And he looked at me,
"My child I have chosen you to be one of my best,
You can't be like everyone else,
You can't run with the rest,
Although you're not perfect,
You live to be like me,
Seeking the good and not the bad,
Living righteously with integrity.
You never were the one that ran to mischief and grief,
You always wanted to do the right thing,
 making me proud of my special seed,
I know its hard being different,
And set apart from the rest,
I know you feel like you have it worse than everyone else,
But hear me my child,
For every test,
 I love you and want to see you blessed."

SEARCHIN'

I seek you Father

To find my life's direction

Praying daily for your guidance and protection

A way for me has been made before the beginning of time

Lead me O Father to the destiny that's mine

Your wishes for me I know not

What is behind the curtain remains veiled.

I believe O God those things are great and

only through you will those things be revealed

I want to be great in you, but greatness has a price

Am I willing to sacrifice so much of my personal life?

The ability to do as I want, whenever I please

Without any eyes watching me

Or fulfill my desires whenever I wish

O God give me a heart for you

To desire to do what you want me to;

To not see it as a burden, but a joy

To take up my cross with no complaint

and live like you want me to live,

To live so that you smile at me consistently

I want to make you proud Lord…

So what's stopping me?

Me.

A NEW DAY

The day explodes onto the scene

Everything is quiet and serene

The cool morning air refreshes my mind as my lungs breathe in

The call of a new day

Can this be the day

Where I finally come together?

Put things into perspective?

Live my life to the fullest?

Believe in the unexpected?

Can this be the day

Where I finally get things right?

Figure out what to do with my life?

Let fate take a shot at me, or

decide on whether it's to be

or not to be?

I don't know what this day will bring

The same ol', same ol' ordinary, everyday things

All one can do is sit there and wait

To see how this day determines my fate.

THOUGHTS THAT RUN AMUCK

A clear, blue sky
A soft gentle breeze
All the ingredients I need to put my mind totally at ease
To leave my thoughts free to run amuck
Sensitivity to my very touch
Cumulous clouds bouncing joyously by
As my eye try to recognize
The beauty that surrounds me
and the peace I feel within
Tall trees that offer shade as the evening comes to an end
A pink and blue horizon lies before me offering tranquil thought
The possibilities are endless, giving me insight into my destiny
My diversity
My unique qualities
That makes me who I am
That special person who has no twin in this cruel and selfish world
Me
The special one
The chosen one
Knowing nothing but greatness
Me
The beautiful creature that I am inside and out
Knowing nothing but love and understanding
Me
Only
Me

Mood:

Sassy

"I was brought up to believe that how I saw myself was more important than how others saw me."

Anwar el-Sadat

Why "DIVA" is my signature piece...

The story of "DIVA" is a very special and moving one. I saw God display his power in a way I'd never seen before. I have coined the year 1997 as "one of the worst years of my life". I experienced a deeply painful break-up, hated my major, and for the first time that I can recall, I was really unsure of myself or what I wanted to do with my life. I'd truly hit an all time low. A friend suggested that I compete in the Miss Texas Southern University pageant.

I knew I had what it took to win. That crown was as good as mine, but there was one thing standing between me and my throne. That doggone swimsuit competition! As confident as I am, there is a monumental difference between hiding girth and imperfections under stylish attire, and displaying all of that which is, and should, remain hidden on stage in front of hundreds of people. As a voluptuous size 24, I wasn't comfortable sashaying around with all my business in the street. I was afraid people would heckle me and make fun of me. I was even discouraged by some well meaning family members that shared the same fears and didn't want to see me hurt. So I prayed about it and God assured me to go for it, fears and all. He later confirmed His words to me through a friend I shared my fear with. My friend told me,

"TaKasha, they may laugh at you, but let them laugh with you. You get up there smiling and strutting your stuff! Have a good time. So even if they do laugh at the "big girl", they'll leave the pageant talking about the "big girl" that rocked it!"

So, I became a Miss TSU contestant. While preparing for the talent portion of the competition I wrote "DIVA". I wanted to do a dramatic piece on strong black women and didn't find anything that suited me. So I decided to write something. I wanted to write something that described me and other strong women I loved and admired. My first thought was of my mother. She's a strong and beautiful woman. She's tough and opinionated, yet loving and kind. She ain't scared of nobody on "two legs or four" as she says, and maintains high morals and standards. The list of her attributes goes on and on, and I wanted this piece to celebrate strong women like my mama and the women in my family. After my initial performance of "DIVA" at the pageant, I received a standing ovation from the crowd and went on to win the pageant! The same people I thought would laugh at me, cheered me on and supported me! Only God can do that!

Thanks to His awesome power, I broke barriers and became the <u>first</u> plus sized queen in the 51 year history of one of the largest historically black universities in the United States! Since my win in 1998, several other plus-sized women have competed and some have won the pageant. This experience always reminds that God can do the unthinkable in our lives if we are obedient, have faith, and trust Him. So what you're about to read is a poem that describes the modern day "Proverbs 31" woman. A beautiful woman, inside and out, who is confident and assured with a no nonsense attitude. A godly woman who knows her worth and possesses strong values and morals. An intelligent woman who possesses her own mind and rejects passive stereotypes of weak women. A "nervy so and so" that doesn't know a thing about "a woman's place". And what do you call this smart, fabulous, beautiful, classy, intelligent sista? What else could a woman like this be? A DIVA!

DIVA

Just the other day, someone threw a question my way,
And asked me what a **DIVA** is supposed to be.
I started to reach for a dictionary, but found it was quite unnecessary,
since you see, this is my area of expertise,
So I sat her down, and told her to heed the words I have spoken,
For although many are called,
Only a few are chosen

A **DIVA** is a woman of distinction,
She stands out in any crowd,
Her presence is so dazzling, you'll treat her like royalty,
And even those of you who hate me, eventually will have to bow down,

A **DIVA** is an individual,
She's not afraid to be who she is
Big, or small, short or tall, confidence is the key by which she lives,
Real beauty lies in the beholder's eyes,
But your beauty is a shame, if you don't have a brain
You'll be impressed by mind and not just my behind,
I'm not your freak or your whore, and definitely not a revolving door.
My first and last name is respect, so don't come here with that mess,
I descend from a lineage of queens so you know what that means,
If you want to be with me you must be ready to be my king

Don't be fooled by this beautiful face
For I will quickly put you in your place, the moment it seems you have lost your mind,
Brother you're not the first or the last and this too shall pass,
So to deal with your stupidity at the present moment would be a waste of my oh, so valuable time,

A **DIVA** you see is a woman of versatility; she blends in well wherever she goes,
So personable and bright others bask in my light and there isn't a person worth knowing that I don't know,

Adored by all I have a ball as I wrap the world around my finger one by one.
Never settling for less, I'm accustomed to only the best while I leave the rest of you
Amazed and stunned,

So let me end this rendition with a short definition of a true **DIVA**'s creed,
I could care less about your insults because in the end result, you don't have to like me,
But you will respect me.
You will respect that like Mary J. Blige I'm not gon' cry when you talk and whisper about me,
I smile and take it as flattery for in most cases it's only jealousy or your subconscious desire to want to be like me,
I'm impressed, when you start your petty mess the way catty little women do,
Cause I'll tell you the truth, you are living proof that you're more concerned about me, than I will ever be about you

So to my **DIVA** sisters in here and all over the world, say "You go Girl!!!", and keep your heads up high,
For it does not matter what they say, you will still succeed anyway, and remember that your only limit is that of the sky!

Mood:

Angry

"He who angers you, controls you."
Unknown

I'm mad as hell today!!!! I'm sick of people f%$#n' with me! I take the high road and ignore their silly asses and they keep it comin'! I let em' make it and they keep on. They don't take the hint and leave me alone. They get worse as if they're daring me to go off. And God won't let me get em' because he told me to let Him fight my battles. But Lord you're taking too long! I've been under so much stress and a lot of it is because I've been holding my peace!

My enemies seem to be winning and I want to fight back. I'm sick of taking the high road. Damn that! I feel like I'm getting punked because God won't let me fight back the way I want to. All some people need is a good ass whoopin' or to get told off and cussed out one good time, and then they'll know not to mess with you. That sh*$ works. Well, I know it doesn't always work like that, but right now, it'll sure as hell make me feel better. I get so tired of operating in integrity because it costs sooooooooooo much. There doesn't seem to be any benefit to doing things right.

When I consider the sacrifices that I've made in an attempt to live righteously, I <u>have</u> to believe that God will restore to me everything I've lost operating in integrity. What have I lost? Relationships, opportunities for promotion, some material wealth, and a slew of other things because I refused to compromise and did "the right thing." Earlier I emphasized "have" because it is a choice that I must make based on my faith. Otherwise, I'm left to operate in the reality that heavily suggests the "good guys finish last" because the road of integrity requires much more and is often travelled alone. Needless to say, I've missed this mark more times than I can count, and I have fallen. However, pastor reminded us through the story of Job to be encouraged because the Lord "knows the way I take" and that He will restore everything I've sacrificed or lost attempting to please Him. That's okay though...God ain't sleep......

GOD AIN'T SLEEP

You may have dug your pit,
Wide and deep,
But you'll fall in yourself,
Because God ain't sleep,

He saw what you did,
His eyes never close,
The evil you inflicted on me that you thought you got away with,
My God in heaven knows,
He saw the thought before it developed in your evil mind,
But he still didn't let what you did kill me
Because my steps were ordered before the beginning of time,
To make me stronger for the work I must do,
To prepare me for enemies worse than you,
To let my light shine in my circumstance,
To testify and encourage someone else
so that the kingdom of God can be enhanced,

You may have dug your pit,
Wide and deep,
But you'll fall in yourself,
Because God ain't sleep,

He heard what you said,
The lies that you tell,
The stories you make up about me straight from the pits of hell,
He was there on your phone, your e-mail and your text,
He was even there on the pew and in the parking lot
When you were keeping up your mess,
He was at your house and in your car, '
When you said those ungodly things intending to leave me scarred
He heard how you tried to curse me because of your envy, jealousy, and your hate,
Conspiring to block my blessings and encouraging others to participate,

But, you may have dug your pit,
Wide and deep,

But you'll fall in yourself,
Because God ain't sleep,

He sees all and He knows all,
So you're not getting away,
Just because he didn't make you pay today, doesn't mean payday isn't on the way,
You laugh and smirk because you're too stupid to be scared,
You've messed with a child of God-one that He loves and for whom he dearly cares,
He let you dig that pit
Because it would be the perfect fit,
The day you fall in it,
And to make you realize,
that a child of God always triumphs,
Because my daddy never closes His eyes,
So,
You may have dug your pit,
Wide and deep,
Now you've fallen in
And are looking up at me
See I told you,
my God wasn't sleep.

THE KNOCKOUT

Ding! Ding! Ding! Ding!
The bell rings and I'm down,
my head is spinnin',
 the ref begins to count,
Your last shot almost took me out
In this first round bout
On the ground I fell
Reeling from that last hit
Couldn't catch my breath fast enough
But I just can't quit
Gotta think
I'm running out of time
That's when I heard the ref say
NINE!!!
Nine times I try to come back like a true self starter
Nine times you knock me back down
Pounding harder
And harder while I gasp for the next breath I take
I close my eyes while the ref screams
EIGHT!!!
Oh great!
Another chance to get back up and reclaim what's mine-
My security, my peace, my pride, my self esteem, my mind
Preparing myself for what's next…
Your next scheme, your next weapon,
Then the voice yells
SEVEN!!!
I'm bettin'
You think I'm over and done
Barely breathing, my life flies by
And I see battles lost and won
And since I'm already down
You pound
On me as I helplessly take your next jeer, your next kick

Somewhere in the distance, I hear the ref yell
SIX!!!
Six minutes
Six minutes
Six minutes
That's it you're on
It's do or die now
If you quit you're gone
You're more than a conqueror
That's what God said in His word
I'm feeling my strength come back and that's when I heard
FIVE!!!
I'm still alive
even though you tried to kill me with evil and strife,
You tried to take my life, but forgot I was walking in "the light"
As the ref says
FOUR!!!
I see the door
Opening
to my renewed strength and might
I see God saying, "I'll be with you always. I already told you this wasn't your fight."
I feel my mind coming back
Strength in my arms and feet
Before I know it, I've struggled to my knees
THREE!!!
I feel free to take on any thing you've got
While you strut around like a proud peacock
The crowd is cheering and you think it's for you
but they're cheering for me
As the ref yells
TWO!!!
I'm standing right behind you
More determined than ever
No longer bound
God give me the strength to knock this sucker down

Give me the strength to deliver this killer blow
Too late devil, you're on the floor
The counting begins again-
 but the difference is
No matter how often I fall
I always win!

Mood: Crunk!

"Decide that you want it more than you're afraid of it."
Bill Cosby

I'm speaking at a student leadership conference in Chicago next week and I'm so stoked! I want to encourage them to be all they can be and empower them beyond their wildest dreams. I'm thinking about using one of my favorite quotes from Bill Cosby- "Decide that you want it more than you're afraid of it." As we get caught up in the rigors of life, we forget about the dreams and purpose God has placed inside of all of us. We become complacent and settle for the comfort of what we know and what we have become accustomed to. We even settle for what we think we deserve, when God has so much more in mind for us. Sadly, we live beneath our purpose for various reasons: fear, families, doubt, physical or emotional limitations, etc. I specifically want to focus on the fear excuse, because I have been personally challenged in that area. Dr. Cosby's quote is one of my favorites because your passion should always surpass your fear of something you really want.

As I've accepted this truth, I've found that indeed my passion has taken over and I truly want what God has for me, more than I'm afraid of it. At one time, I was afraid of what God was showing me I was capable of with <u>Him</u>. Oddly, I was not afraid to fail, but to succeed. I was afraid of the enormous responsibility that accompanies greatness. I didn't want to disappoint God or myself. However, I've learned that getting started truly is the hardest part. Once you start, it becomes easier to get to your purposed place! Whether it's a career promotion, educational goal, or simply to lose weight, or become a better person, GO GET IT! Hmmm... that's a good place to start. Let me see what I can do with that.....

GO GET IT!!

Go get it!
Stop wanting and wishing and waiting on it.
Keep it on your mind and go to work every day on it.
You've got the stuff,
Go head and flaunt it!
Stop talkin' about it and act like you want it!
Go get it!
It's waiting just for you
All you have to do
is make it "do what it do"
 and see it through,
to the end,
You're empowered to win!
God gave you what you need
so that's where you begin,
And once you begin
Don't stop,
you belong at the top
Whether other people or you think so or not
You've got to use what you've got,
To take you higher,
And once you get there baby its gon' be fire,
Too hot to handle,
too cold to hold,
You're in control,
keep reaching for your goal
and
<u>GO GET IT</u>!!!!!

I SEE IT!!

I see it
What you said I couldn't be
I see it
What you thought wasn't for me
I see it
Clearer than the clearest day
I see it
It's looming closer
On its way
I see it
No more doubt and no more fear
I see it
No longer fuzzy in my mind
But crystal clear
I see it
Though you counted me out and laughed at me
I see it
Being everything God made me to be
I see it
It doesn't matter if you do
I see it
What was once a dream
Is now a dream come true
I see it
No matter what obstacles are in my way
God told me I can have it!
That's why I go to work on it every day
It's in my spirit!
<u>NO ONE</u> can take it away,
I see it
I see it
I believe it
I believe it
I believe it

IT IS SO!!!!!!!!!!

AND SO WE COMMENCE

And so we commence
To heights unknown
Heads held high
Our past behind us
Our dreams to the sky
Going forward in god's vision
His will for me
Being everything He ordained and created me to be
And so we commence
To the next level, He has for me
Steadfast and walking in the victory
Doing what some said couldn't be done
Praising Him for victories already won
Forging ahead until my work is done
So we stand here today
In postures of praise and war
Ready for whatever the devil thinks he has in store
And so we commence
And so they commence
One by one,
our heads held high
Because we've already won!

Mood:

Depressed

"Doubt is a pain too lonely to know that faith is his twin brother."
Khalil Gibran

Life is funny. Everyday I wake up I think to myself that you never know what surprises God has in store for you that day. Things aren't great right now and I'm a little down. I'd planned for certain things in my life to pan out a much differently. These past few weeks, I've been plagued with frustration. In some instances, things haven't gelled together as I'd planned or as quickly as I'd planned. I've felt abandoned by God concerning things He promised me in His Word about His vision for me and several other areas of my life. I know what He told me, and while I get weary, I'm not going to give up. I am NOT a quitter. But when Satan knows that no matter how weary we get, we will not quit, He attacks us by keeping us ensnared in distractions and obstacles. While contemplating this thought, I was reminded of Henry Ford's words, "Obstacles are those frightful things you see when you take your eyes off your goal."
This modernized take on Paul's admonishment in the New Testament to "forget those things that are behind us and press toward the mark of a higher calling" has re-ignited my faith and resolve to see God's vision through no matter what. My faith is renewed and I anticipate the manifestation of His promises since He cannot lie. So since I'm feeling this way, have I just been lying to myself?

ACCEPT

Accept
that the only person who can change things is you
Accept
That things are exactly as God knew they would be at this time
Accept
That life is not fair and sometimes quite f'ed up
Accept
That things won't go as you'd planned
Accept
That every day is a new opportunity for things to be different
Accept
Those friends are few,
 acquaintances soon fade,
and bull comes a dime a dozen
Accept
That everyone will not like you,
Some will tolerate you,
very few will love you
Accept
That you are not every woman and cannot be all things to all people
Accept
That some people are crutches you keep around because you're too weak to face your real issues
Accept
That things won't get better until you change your mind
Accept
That it's easier to be in the will of God, but harder to stay in it
Accept
That it doesn't always have to be like this
Accept
That some people glory in your sadness because it makes them feel better
Accept

that you must love yourself and see you as God sees you
Accept
That it is what it is and living in the past benefits no one, especially you.
Accept
That longsuffering really means you "suffer long"
Accept
That you are exactly where you need to be whether you think so or not,
or whether you like it or not
Accept it
Because it won't change.

Mood: Reflective

A tribute to my great grandmother
Ms. Luetta Katie Owens
February 8, 1914- April 12, 2008

My great grandmother is one of the most important people in my life. She's ninety-four years old and we've always been close. She's such a strong woman of God. I love talking to her because she's so wise. I'm amazed that I can talk to her about most things and she understands. I guess I sometimes forget that she was once a young woman too. She introduced me to God as a young child with nightly prayers and we often read the bible together. She taught me to pray and always reminded me that "God is Love". I often think about how I'm living off her stored up prayers for me and I thank her for it. As a people our ancestry dictates our greatness. From Kings and Queens that birthed civilizations, to slaves that birthed and built this nation, to freedom fighters putting their lives on the line for equality, to modern day movers of the struggle in this generation called "Me". I'm so proud to walk in the awesome path she has carved for me. Her legacy is truly one of faith-believing God for everything. Grandmama has always possessed a quiet strength clothed in a meek spirit. Although she's been through so much, her head was never bowed, except in prayer. I want to leave that kind of great legacy of my own for my nephew and children to see. With God's help, I will.

LEGACY

Looking back
I see
So much of what I am expected to be
 The glory
The legacy
But I've still gotta be me
Looking back
I see
The past littered with triumph and acclaim
The glory of another person's name
But our names are not the same
Looking back I see
A portrait of high self esteem
People who look like me
Realizing dreams they thought they could never see
Achieving heights unsurpassed by ma-ny
But where does that leave me?
Looking forward
I guess
Not deterred by the rest
Striving to be the best
My calling
My des-tin-y
Looking forward
It's true
That I don't have to be like you
To do what you do
I can learn and achieve, and earn the same respect, only diff'rent-ly
Looking forward I shine
With superior legacy following close behind.
On my heels as I succeed, achieve, and dream
Oh what an honor to carve out my own legacy!!!!!!
Keeping your legacy alive without breaking my own stride,
Learning from proven success
As I evolve from good, to better, to best!

ENJOYING THE JOURNEY

When I look back over my life
I've had some misery and strife
But there was a lot I ran into
that I didn't have to go through
Because someone like you
Had been there to
Because what we go through is never just for self
But for someone else
I'm just glad to have had your invaluable help
When I was crossing that ocean, or swimming that sea
You were there for me
because you'd swam across them previously,
Or when I was climbing that mountain, the one you'd told to move long ago
Or when I was taking that test,
 the one you passed with flying colors because you had
been there, done that, bought the t-shirt... and, well you know the rest
Or maybe the time, I asked your advice
Before making some of the most important decisions in my life
And you safely guided me through, because you'd been there too
Ahhhh... the mistakes I never made, the hurts I never felt,
the lessons I didn't have to learn the hard way,
the new experiences I can now share with someone else!
So looking back, I have few regrets,
and without you I know I couldn't do it
So as I approach another test,
 because God only tests His best,
I can proudly say,
"I didn't have to go through it,
because I knew it,
before I got to it!"

I can't believe she's gone. She died at 6:30 this morning. I'm glad it was peaceful and she's at rest now. These last two weeks have been emotionally, physically, and spiritually trying because I've been watching my grandmama die. When she went into the hospital two weeks ago, I was worried because something felt different this time. I couldn't place it at the time, but I felt like she may not pull through. Now, I know it was God mercifully preparing me. Call it crazy but I thought she would outlive all of us. The thought of life without her was inconceivable to me because she'd been with me my entire life.

For two weeks, I watched her cry and pray aloud for Jesus to have mercy on her and not to let her die in pain. Sometimes I thought her mind was going because of some of the things she said. Not to mention, she talked about seeing dead relatives like her mother and Aunt Alice. I remember walking in her hospital room one day after court, and when she saw me she started crying. I was stunned because I'd never seen Grandmama cry, even when Aunt Alice died. I was so heartbroken because I felt completely helpless. There was nothing I could do about her pain and suffering. At that moment she looked like a helpless child...the child I once was that cried out to her. She was a proud woman and not used to being confined in bed with a catheter. She'd been asking to go to the bathroom all day because although her body was weak, her mind was strong. I gently explained to her that she wasn't strong enough to get up and walk around yet, but we'd try it if she wanted to. Although she struggled for nearly 3 minutes or so to simply sit up because she was too weak to stand, I marveled at her stubborn resolve. That night she sat up without assistance for about 45 minutes, and she was happy.

As I endured this emotional ebb and flow, I prayed for her healing but the reality was settling in that she was going to die. While visiting her one night, she looked at me as if she could read my thoughts, and told me to pray for the family and not to grieve for her. It was as if she also knew her time with us was coming to a close. I cried like a baby because her words confirmed the uneasy feeling I felt. I prayed and asked God for peace and strength but then I prayed the unthinkable-for God's will to be done and to give me the strength to accept His will no matter what it is. That is one of the hardest prayers to pray, and I know it was the Holy Spirit interceding for me. I wanted God to heal her and I wanted more time with her. I wanted her to witness my wedding day, just as she'd witnessed violin recitals, beauty pageants, and graduations. I wanted my unborn children to know the woman who loved and nurtured me throughout my life and experience her unyielding love for them, just as I had. I wanted to be able to still sit at her feet and partake in her wisdom.

But a good friend reminded me that while you're praying for God to grant you peace and strength, pray that He will also incline His ear to her requests. If it's time for

Him to take her home, that He would be merciful and not let her suffer. Once I started praying along these lines, my reasons for wanting her here with me, paled in comparison to my love for her. I knew she was tired and ready to be with Jesus. She was only holding on for us because she knew we weren't ready for her to go. I'd reached a point where her peace was more important. And now, that's where she is...at peace in the bosom of Jesus. I never knew anyone who loved the Lord as much. She accepted Christ early in life, lived for Him, and taught us to know and love Him.

When I think of my grandmama, her legacy to me wasn't one of material riches, although she lived comfortably. She wasn't hindered by her fourth grade education or the fact that her employment history started in Louisiana sugar cane, cotton, and pecan fields, and ended as a housekeeper. She never knew what it meant to earn $20,000 a year, yet she raised several children, never lived in debt, and maintained college funds for all of her grandchildren and great-grandchildren. I'm so proud to have that kind of strength running through my veins. Her legacy is that she gave me the best gift of all- she introduced me to Jesus Christ. Because of her, I know Him and love Him.

This hurts so much. Since her death, I literally have to take life one day at a time. I've been throwing myself into my work so I don't have to think about it as much. But I'm sure that will catch up to me sooner or later. I don't want to "feel" right now. I don't know how I'm going to feel when I wake up in the morning. Sometimes I wake up crying, or tear up throughout the day. Sometimes, the tears don't fall, but my soul cries. It's the weirdest feeling to want to cry and can't. It's a heaviness that's indescribable because the pain is so deep. People say it gets easier with time, and I hope it does. I remember the day she died. It was a beautiful Saturday. I sat in her room for hours just staring at her lifeless body. Strangely enough, she just looked like she was asleep. I sprinkled her face with kisses and I kept waiting for her to wake up. But she didn't. It was surreal- a significant part of me is no longer here with me and the emptiness is too much to bear at times. But while her death deeply grieves me, I praise God for her life, her wisdom, and for the love she has imparted in my life and the lives of others. In the meantime though, I just need God's strength to live on...

I WATCHED YOU SLEEP

I watched you sleep
So peaceful and serene
Seeming not to have a care in mind
And as I stared
I found comfort there
Even though you'd reached the end of your time

I watched you sleep
So peaceful and serene
And I waited for you to wake up
To open your eyes and smile at me
To go back to the way things used to be,
When you were breathing

I watched you sleep
And it dawned on me
That you were transitioning
That sleeping is all you'll ever do
And I'll never again look upon you humanly
Now all I have are beautiful memories
As I watched you sleep
I noticed how you never stirred or moved
I slowly began to realize
That the last time
I saw you
Was to be the last time I'd ever see you
Over here on this side
The last smile I'd ever see
The last words you'd ever speak to me
The last time you'd look upon me
Lovingly
The last hug I'd ever feel
The last time we'd share a meal
The last time I'd hear you say, you loved me

All because you went to sleep
Peacefully and blissfully
Without confusion or bickering
Pain or suffering
Jesus came you see
And rescued you from your misery
Took you out of that hospital robe and old clothes
And gave you a new white robe, lined with gold
He gave you a new indestructible body
Free of sickness and disease
And while your slumber deeply saddens me
and hurts me badly
I rejoice gladly
knowing you're now safe in His arms,
The only place you'd rather be,
Than here with me.
So, I'll watch you sleep
Peaceful and serene
And while it grieves me deeply
I'm letting fond memories
Not tempt me
To grieve for too long,
Because if I do
What I'm supposed to
I'll be just like you
On that great getting' up mornin'
When God calls me home.

Mood:

Introspective

"Remember no one can make you feel inferior without your consent."
Eleanor Roosevelt

I remember watching "The Burning Bed" as a child. I recall watching those horrible beatings, flinching, and thinking how sad it is to live like that. I also remembered how empowered Farrah Fawcett's character was after she killed her abusive husband. Since then domestic violence has intrigued me which is why I'm taking this class. Like most people I've often wondered why women stay in abusive relationships. When I've seen them on talk shows, lots of them say they stay out of love for their abuser, or for their children which is crazy as hell to me. I'm thinking to myself "Just leave, pick up the pieces and go!" How can you think someone who hits you loves you? Granddaddy always said that a man who hits you doesn't love you. Abusive men don't go around hitting themselves for the obvious reason they shouldn't hit anyone else- it hurts. But this class is teaching me that there is more to the story than we think...

A BATTERED WOMAN'S PLIGHT

"Weak" is what you see when you look at me
And maybe you might be right
But until you've walked in my shoes
And took every bruise
you'll never understand a battered woman's plight.

I know what you're thinking
You say it can't be true
Because aside from the fact that I'm black and blue,
 I look and act just like you
The truth is you could be me with all your degrees,
or your GED and still get knocked to your knees
The slap in your face could care less about your race
And staring down the barrel of a 12 gauge disregards your age
"Why does she stay?" is the universal inquiry
It's too easy to leave
She must like getting beat
There are too many shelters and hotlines for her to use
With all that help, she deserves the abuse
But the hotlines are pointless, and all they do
Is direct me to shelters that don't have any room
Have nowhere to go and safely retreat
because my friends and family is the first place he'll come to look for me
He's obsessed, he's deranged, he's out of control
He promised to kill me if I ever tell a soul
So I'm damned if I do and damned if I don't
I'm dead if I leave and dead if I won't
The law can't help me,
The police don't answer the calls,
I've received restraining and protective orders and he's broken them all

So what are my options? Live my life in fear?

Constantly running and looking over my shoulder
Hoping the coast is clear
Well not anymore
I'm taking back my life
By now I hope you understand a battered woman's plight

Since nobody anywhere can give me some help
I'll take matters into my own hands and help myself
I am tired of living life with no peace
And the only way I'll have peace
 is if you are deceased
I'm not waitin' on nature,
my .38 will do just fine
I am taking your life before you take mine
I'm tired of your threats, your stalking, and beatings
Your lies as you apologize
and promise never to do that to me
I'm tired of your fists smashing into my face
Your ugly words that even time cannot erase
You've broken my spirit,
you've destroyed everything you could
I tried to love you anyway, but it didn't do any good
So now I'm fed up and I've had enough
I'm now just like you
Got nothing to lose
Go ahead and be smug
Ignore what I say
You come one step closer,
I'll blow you away

"Vengeful" is what you now see when you look at me
And maybe you might be right
But until you've walked in my shoes
and took every bruise
you'll never understand a battered woman's plight.

"Guilty" is the verdict
But it doesn't make any sense
How could I be guilty of killing a man in self defense?
Does it matter that I escaped and he continued stalking me?
Why didn't you take into account that I repeatedly asked him to leave??
What was I supposed to do when he called in the middle of the night?
How should I have reacted when he stabbed me with his knife?
How did he become the victim, wasn't I the victim first?
Where were you hypocrites when I needed you to protect me from my hurt?
How dare you expect me to take it?
Haven't you heard a word I've just said?
It seemed the only way you'll help me
is if I'm already dead
I'm not glad but I don't feel bad about what I had to do
I had no other choice
Now I'm serving 12 to 22

Whatever you see when you look at me
May or may not be right
But until you've walked in my shoes
and took every bruise
you'll never understand a battered woman's plight.

A TRIBUTE TO THE LOVELY SORORS OF DELTA SIGMA THETA SORORITY!!!!!!

(and a challenge to those aspiring...)

Oo-oop my sorors!

Oo-oop!!!!!

SO YOU WANT TO BE A DELTA?

In the beginning, there were twenty-two
Women of vision
with a purpose for me and you
twenty-two who were not to afraid to say
That Delta Sigma Theta is the only way
So you want to be a Delta?
But do you really know what it takes?
You see it's not about how cute you think you are
Or how fast your behind shakes
It's not about the parties, and it's not about the frat
It's not about being "Greek",
because before you were "Greek", you were "Black"
It's about unity, love, sisterhood, and service to the community
So is "Delta material" who you are
Or merely who you hope to be?
You see Delta women are dynamic divas
Divine and unique
Classy, sassy, and always jazzy
They bring a smile to all they meet
Deltas are excellent!
There's no room for the mediocre
Always rising to the top
Delta women cannot be stopped
For she is the best "womanhood" has to offer
Delta women are leaders
and always on top of their game
If you don't believe me, or simply forgot,
here are some of their names
Barbara Jordan, Shirley Chisholm, and Lena Horne just to name a few,
Dorothy Height, Nikki Giovanni, and Cicely Tyson too
Let's not forget those change agents of the 60's,
and those dynamic women of the arts,
Those politicians, educators, entertainers, doctors, and lawyers

with Delta in their hearts.
A Delta woman is a total woman at best
Never needing anything more,
and never lacking anything less
The essence of womanhood
Compassionate, loyal and true
A sister in need, dedicated to her community,
a true friend indeed,
And faithful through and through
A Delta woman is admired and respected
She stands out wherever she goes
And although some may spite her,
Others want to be just like her
Because without a word,
her beauty and majesty automatically shows
So you want to be a Delta?
After all what else is there to be?
A Delta woman is who I am
Now, do you want to be like me?

Thank you for purchasing your copy of

"The Diva's Diary-Original poetic thought notes and commentary on love and life-Volume I"!

Now that you know the Diva's secrets, don't keep it to yourself! The best secrets are those shared among friends, so tell a friend!

Additional copies of this book can be purchased at:

www.thevoicecommunications.com

To book a speaking engagement or to reach TaKasha L. Francis, please e-mail us at thevoicecom@gmail.com or visit us at www.myspace.com/thevoicecommunications.